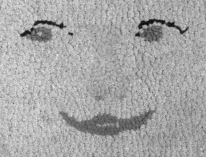

RAG RUGS
OF ENGLAND AND
AMERICA

Geordie Ha'ad the Bairn, a print of an English painting of about 1890 by Ralph Hedley. It was painted from life and shows a miner called Snowdon Pyle in his pit cottage outside Newcastle. The furnishings, complete with "clippie" rug, are typical of the time and show the way that handmade rugs were used to warm and brighten the bare floors of poor houses like this.

Cover Hooked rug from New England c.1835 (detail). 31x74in/79x188cm (see also p. 21)

Endpapers Hooked rug, *Night and Day*, designed by Winifred Nicholson (detail) and made by Mary Bewick in Cumbria mid-1970s. 34x49in/87x125cm

THE DECORATIVE ARTS LIBRARY

RAG RUGS
OF ENGLAND AND
AMERICA

By

Emma Tennant

WALKER BOOKS

LONDON

To Toby

Series Editors

Mirabel Cecil and Rosemary Hill

First published 1992 by Walker Books Ltd
87 Vauxhall Walk, London SE11 5HJ

Distributed in all countries outside North America by
Antique Collectors' Club
5 Church Street, Woodbridge, Suffolk IP12 1DS, UK
tel: 01394 385501 fax: 01394 384434

Distributed in North America by
Antique Collectors' Club
Market Street Industrial Park, Wappingers' Falls, NY 12590, USA
tel: 800 252 5231 fax: 914 297 0068

Text © 1992 Emma Tennant
Illustrations on pages 32-3 © 1992 Patrick Benson

Printed and bound in Hong Kong by
South China Printing Co. (1988) Ltd

British Library Cataloguing in Publication Data
A catalogue record for this book is
available from the British Library
ISBN 0-7445-1892-X

Contents

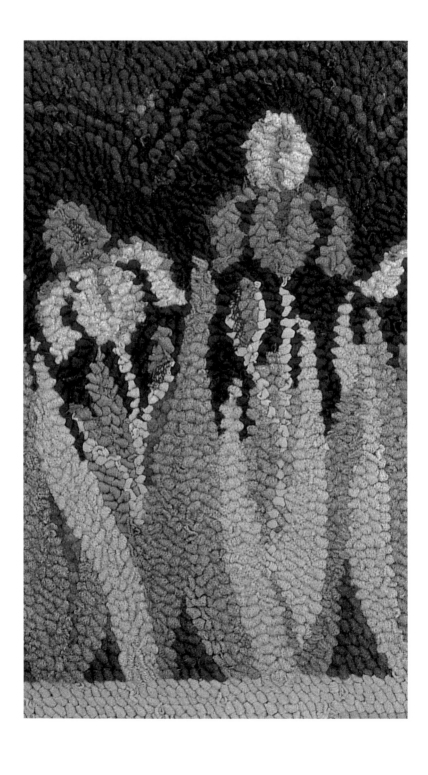

-Editors' Preface-

The rag rugs in this book were made by women, most of them now unknown, from the stuff of their everyday lives. The best designs were their own, uninfluenced by anything except the view through their windows which they translated into rugs in the humble medium of rags – their childrens' worn out clothes, their husbands' breeches. The flowers in a vase on the kitchen table might be turned into a rug from an old flannel petticoat whose cheerful scarlet would become the petals of a poppy.

Rag rug-making over the last two centuries – the period covered by this book – has been chiefly the work of women, but they relied on men to make the simple equipment, hooks and wooden frames for stretching the backing, and indeed to provide much of their material, from old uniforms to fishing nets. These rug-makers were not trained in anything – except patience; they could fit in their rugging at home while waiting for the men to come back from the fields, the war, or the sea, or their children from school.

For women in many different communities – farmers' wives in mid-nineteenth-century America and Britain or fishermens' wives in impoverished Labrador – rug-making satisfied the same needs: it brought colour into austere homes and occupied long winter evenings of rural isolation. It offered a chance to earn some money, or to immortalize the family cat, and a taste of independence, economic or artistic.

Some designs are crude, others fine; some colours are sombre, some bright. The best rugs are still amusing, like the tumbling caribou on page 74, or touching, like the simple "proggies" made by miners' wives in the north-east of England. On both sides of the Atlantic rug-makers are continuing the tradition and in Britain Emma Tennant is a leader of the current revival.

Irises by Emma Tennant (detail), 1985. 24x36in/61x91cm

-A Note about Technique-

Rag rug-making – like all crafts – has developed its own vocabulary of curious and specialized terms. A full list of these can be found at the back of the book, but the main technical distinction to bear in mind is between hooked and poked mats. Hooking is worked with the backing stretched on a frame using long strips of fabric to form a closely-looped, smooth surface; a poked rug can be made without a frame and involves pushing short lengths of material through the backing cloth to give a shaggier pile. The two techniques are sometimes combined, with many regional and personal variations.

Rug-making tools: often adapted to suit the individual rugger, the names and styles vary from place to place.

Zodiac hooked rug by the Welsh rug-maker Jenni Stuart-Anderson. The figures are taken from fifteenth-century woodcuts, 1990. 42in/106cm diameter

-The United States of America-

O f all the ways the thrifty American housewife had of making "something new from something old", rug-hooking became the most popular and the most enduring. The earliest rugs or "ruggs" were used – as they were in Europe – for bedcovers, and bed rugs continued to be made until about 1830; they were yarn sewn on linen backgrounds. Not until 1810 does the *Oxford English Dictionary* have a reference to "a little rug for your hearthstone".

Homer Eaton Keyes, the first editor of the American magazine *Antiques*, wrote in 1925: "the history of hooked rugs is buried so deeply beneath unsubstantial tradition and romantic legend as almost to defy efforts to unearth reliable fragments."

Since then there has been much speculation and controversy about where the technique originated and this book cannot hope to resolve the question. It is written, however, on the premise that rag rug-making was a European tradition, taken to North America by settlers who developed it and who, with their descendants, brought about the finest flowering of the craft.

The first American hooked rugs were made on the eastern seaboard: in Maine, New Hampshire and across the Canadian

Patriotic themes were a source of inspiration, especially during the Civil War when this rug was made. 25x42in/63x107cm

border in New Brunswick, Nova Scotia, Prince Edward Island, in areas of French-speaking Quebec and on north to New-foundland and Labrador. By the end of the nineteenth century hooked rugs were made all over North America.

Most of the early settlers on the north-eastern seaboard came from northern Europe, in particular the British Isles. They brought with them their religion and traditions. Their way of life in the nineteenth century, based on fishing and farming, was hard, with no money to spare for luxuries and long, cold winters to endure. In Colonial times, such carpets as people had were imported, and very expensive. When factory-made carpets were first produced domestically in the 1820s, they were still

The trotting horse was a popular theme in nineteenth-century folk art. A weathervane, or a painting on glass like the one shown below, might have served as a model for the spirited, if somewhat ungainly, pony on the rug (*left*). Both date from the second half of the nineteenth century. 32x51in/81x130cm

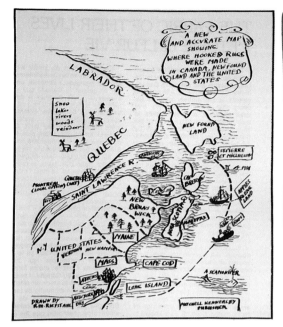

This map illustrated an auction catalogue advertising the sale of a collection of hooked rugs in 1923 in New York. This was the height of the craze for rug collecting among sophisticated city-dwellers.

beyond the means of all but the wealthy.

Most families depended on home-produced wool and linen for clothing and for furnishing their houses. Their textiles were spun, woven and dyed at home, and they were far too valuable to waste. Every last scrap, and the least worn parts of old clothes, were saved and re-used – the cotton for patchwork quilts, the woollen for rugs.

The introduction of burlap (known as hessian in Britain and as brin in parts of Canada) was a great fillip to rug-making, because it provided an ideal cheap, durable backing. Burlap was made from Indian jute and by the mid-nineteenth century large quantities were being imported into North America, where it was used for sacks; the dimensions of the sacks opened out, washed and stretched on a frame, dictated the size of the rug.

The designs on the earliest rugs were drawn freehand at home.

Cats, traditionally guardians of the hearth, have always been favourite subjects for rugs. This pair dates from the second half of the nineteenth century; the loops have been sheared to give a velvety pile. 34x57in/86x145cm

People naturally turned to their immediate surroundings and depicted what they knew best. Their naïve designs may often be crudely drawn, but they have vitality and charm and show some attempt at symmetry. Some are so sophisticated as to rival the French carpets that inspired them. Flowers, arranged in a vase or basket, leaves and fruit were the commonest subjects. They were often framed in a border of simple rows in a contrasting colour, or decorated with curving leaves and tendrils.

On farms and in small towns where rug-making flourished, life revolved round animals and crops. The horse was supremely important and dogs and cats too worked for their keep. They

Hooked rug from New England *c.*1835 (*above*). 31x74in/79x188cm

Most rug designs are based on familiar subjects. This exotic beast may have been inspired by a print, possibly from Bewick's *Quadrupeds*, published in Philadelphia in 1810 (*left*). 41x67in/104x170cm

all found their way into the rug-makers' repertoire, along with other animals, including beavers (especially in Canada), foxes, ducks, geese, chickens and cattle.

The seafaring life of the coast was also a rich source of ideas. Ships in full sail, fishing boats, whales, anchors, ropes, shells and lighthouses are all illustrated on rugs, probably made by sailors or by their wives or sweethearts. The best of them convey the effects of sky and sea by clever use of line and colour.

One of three famous rugs made in about 1860 by Lucy Barnard of Dixfield Common, Maine. It shows her favourite horse, Betsy. 36x65in/91x165cm

Ambitious subjects, such as houses and landscapes, were not beyond the scope of the most skilled rug-makers. Variations on these range from simple box-like buildings to the famous set of three large rugs made by Lucy Barnard in the mid-nineteenth century, one of which is illustrated on pages 22-3. Interior scenes were less common, perhaps because the rugs were made during the long, dark winter months. Part of the pleasure of depicting flowers, fruit and summery landscapes

Rug-makers often copied designs from more expensive types of carpet. This one (*right*) is based on a Turkish design. Mid-nineteenth century. 76x83in/193x211cm

Patterns were sometimes taken from patchwork as in this harmonious composition of flowers on a geometric background (*below*). Late nineteenth century. 60x74in/152x188cm

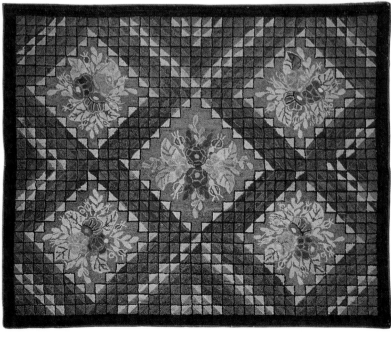

was to bring them indoors permanently. When all was dark and snowy outside, nothing could be more cheering than bright flowers on the hearthrug.

Yet another source of inspiration was patriotism. The American Eagle and the Stars and Stripes were both symbolic and attractive and, as in England, old army uniforms made perfect background material.

The vocabulary of patchwork quilts was easily adapted to rug-hooking. The well-known *Log Cabin* and *Baby Blocks* patterns were often used. So were designs with curves and circles, such as the overlapping clamshell pattern drawn by outlining cups or plates. Abstract designs based on geometric patterns are found in all rug-making areas: the simplest of them is a random selection of colours worked in lines which can be straight or wavy, giving a marbled effect. It is called "hit or miss" in America, "scrappie" in Canada and "mizzy-mazzy" in parts of England. Even this most basic design can be very pleasing when it is given shape by a firm outline of black or another dark colour.

Persian and Turkey rugs, fashionable in well-off households from the middle of the eighteenth century, were often copied in hooked form, but the results are dull and predictable unless the maker had an exceptional eye for colour. Different kinds of design were often combined in one rug. Bunches of flowers may have geometric borders, dogs are embowered in branches, lions sit in a garden and horses trot through a mosaic sky.

Even when they have faded, the colours of many old hooked rugs are still attractive. The earliest makers depended on vegetable dyes and the list of plants they used is long. Hemlock bark, yellow hickory, peach leaves, walnut or spruce bark, golden rod, onion skins, sumac, sassafras, blueberry ... dozens of plants produced a wide range of colours. Brown came from the

butternut tree (*Juglans cinerea*); so many Confederate soldiers were dressed in home-spun dyed with it that the nickname "Butternut" stuck to them for many years after the Civil War. Synthetic dyes, which made harsher, brighter colours available, were introduced in the 1860s.

The loops of American hooked rugs were often cut, or "sheared", after they were finished. Sometimes the length of the pile was varied as well, giving a sculptured effect. One Dalmatian dog design made in this way has a furry coat three

This lion may have been made in Canada, as beavers are included in the design. Second half of the nineteenth century. 33x60in/84x152cm

inches long. These rugs are known as Waldoboro-type, from the town of Waldoboro, Maine, where the technique was first developed. Many of them consist of brightly-coloured wreaths or baskets of flowers on dark backgrounds, and they are often hooked on linen.

The rug-makers did not have to rely entirely on home-drawn designs. They could also copy craftsmen's interpretations of favourite motifs. The tinsmith's horse or cockerel on the weathervane is sometimes so similar to the woollen version of the same subject that it seems it was used as a template. The favourite New England sport of trotting was illustrated in paintings, and in training manuals whose fine steel engravings showing the horses' gait were easy to copy. The popular fashion for stencilled decoration on walls and furniture provided another source of patterns that could be adapted to the cruder medium of hooked rugs, and what was lost in subtle detail was often gained in bold vitality.

Innovations were gradually made in the design of hooks. At first they had been improvised at home, in the farm workshop or by the local blacksmith, out of an old nail, a key or a tool such as a gimlet – which had the advantage of a comfortable wooden handle. In 1886 Ebenezer Ross of Toledo, Ohio, invented a "Novelty Rug Machine", a sort of punch or shuttle hook, to speed up the hooking. It was the first of several gadgets designed to make the work quicker and easier.

An advertisement from *Lippincott's Monthly Magazine* of 1887.

From *Scribner's Magazine*, 1889.

In the 1850s the first commercially produced rug patterns were made in Lowell, Massachusetts. They were die-stamped on hessian using large wooden printing blocks with inlaid copper designs. (See rug and printing blocks on right.)

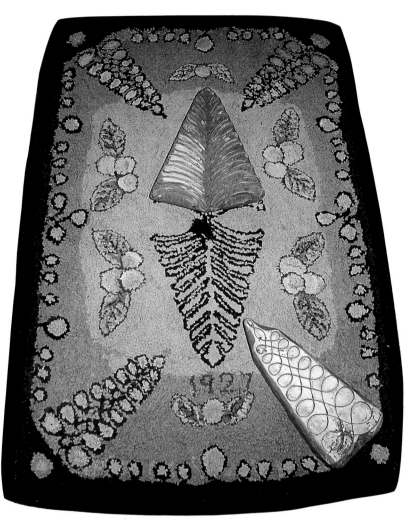

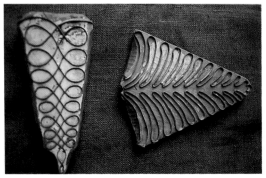

Frost the Rug Man

The best-known ready-made designs were those produced by Edward Sands Frost between 1868 and 1876. Frost was a one-time mechanic who had been invalided out of the army in 1863. He returned home to Biddeford, Maine, and earned his living as a pedlar of tinware. He described in his memoirs how his wife went about making a rag rug. An artistic cousin drew out a design on hessian for her; she sewed it to her quilting frame and

began work with a hook made from an old nail. Frost watched her.

"I noticed she was using a very poor hook, so, being a machinist, I went to work and made the crooked hook ... which is still in vogue today.

"I caught the fever ... every evening I worked on the rug ... and it was while thus engaged that I first conceived the idea of working up an article that is today about as staple as cotton cloth and sells the world over. Every lady that ever made a rug knows

A modified version of a Frost design. The *Dalmatian* was his pattern No. 150 but the border has been taken from another source. Second half of the nineteenth century. 35x58in/89x147cm

Rural American interiors, like the imaginary one shown on the following page, achieved cheerful decorative effects simply, with rag rugs and stencils.

that it is very pleasant and bewitching to work on a pretty design, but tiresome and hard on plain figure. I told my wife I thought I could make a better design myself than that we were at work on. I wrote my first design on paper and then put it on to the burlap and worked the flower and scroll all ready for the ground work.

"I got orders for twenty or more like it within three days. I put in my time evenings and stormy days sketching designs as the orders came in faster than I could fill them. I began, Yankee-like, to study some way to do them quicker. Then the first idea of stencilling presented itself to me.

"Did I go to Boston to get my stencils made? Oh no, I went out to the stable where I had some old iron and some old wash boilers I had bought for their copper bottoms, took the old tin off them and made my first stencil out of it. I forged my tools to cut the stencils with. I made a cutting block out of old lead and zinc.

"I began making small stencils of single flowers, scrolls, leaves, buds, etc. Then I could with a stencil brush print in ink in plain figures much faster than I could sketch. Thus I reduced ten hours' labor to two and a half hours. I began to print patterns and put them in my peddler's cart and offer them for sale. The news of my invention of stamped rugs spread like magic – I became known as Frost the rug man."

Later, Frost began printing in colour, making it as easy to follow a design from his catalogue as to paint a picture by numbers. "The question of how to print them in colors so as to sell them at a profit seemed to be the point on which the success of the whole business hung. In March 1870, one morning about two o'clock, I seemed to hear a voice in my room say – 'Print your bright colors first and then the dark ones.' That settled it... I sold my tin-peddling business and hired a room in the building

A typical Edward Sands Frost design. His patterns made it easier to work a rug, but the end result was sometimes stiffer and more predictable than the home-designed versions. Second half of the nineteenth century. 35x67in/89x170cm

on Main Street where I began in April 1870 to print patterns in colors."

Frost's health gave way again in 1876 and he sold the business. But his story ended happily. He was carried on a stretcher to California and, when he recovered, invested successfully in land. He died in 1894, a rich man.

Frost's stencils were sold after his death and continued to be available by mail-order until 1900. They now belong, all four tons of them, to the Henry Ford Museum at Greenfield Village, Dearborn, Michigan. Frost cut nearly seven hundred and fifty different stencils which made about one hundred and eighty complete rug designs. They vary from traditional floral types, usually consisting of an oval centrepiece with symmetrical flowered bor-

ders, to what the catalogue described as "elegant Turkish designs, copied from the latest and most desirable importations of Turkish rugs. A perfect imitation both in design and colouring."

The best-known Frost designs are based on animals: spaniels, Dalmatians, stags, horses, cats and a bird on its nest in a wreath of flowers. Most are neatly framed with foliage, ropes or scrolls. The lion, one of Frost's most popular patterns, sometimes has an exotic background of palm trees.

There is no doubt that rugs made with these stamped designs lack the originality and vitality that distinguish the best naïve examples. Luckily, many people did not feel bound to follow the printed patterns too closely. By adding their own details and improvisations they gave individuality to the finished article. In any case, the use of different rags and scraps means that no two hooked rugs are ever identical.

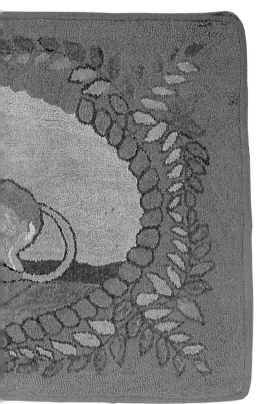

A Frost design showing a typical combination of central motif and a floral border. Second half of the nineteenth century. 26x35in/67x90cm

Edward Sands Frost pattern No. 160. Second half of the nineteenth century. 26½x35½in/67x90cm

Themes and Variations

The Shakers, the nineteenth-century religious sect chiefly remembered now for their skill as craftsmen and designers, had, typically, their own style of rug design. Their philosophy of craftsmanship "perfect for purpose" made them sympathetic to the thrifty idea of using rags to make rugs, and they devoted the same careful attention to this humble craft as to all their other activities.

They made them using a variety of methods, in particular "dollar mats", in which circles of cloth about the size of a silver dollar were cut out with a gadget like a pastry-cutter and sewn to a backing. Most of these seem to date from the first half of the nineteenth century. Later on the Shakers made hooked rugs

which they often finished off with a characteristic braided border. They also made "shag mats" by pulling strips through a knitted backing, exactly as miners' wives did in England when hessian was unobtainable during the First World War. The Shaker designs include two famous horse rugs, but they were usually geometric abstract patterns.

With the twentieth century, styles changed as well as techniques. Human figures, rarely seen on nineteenth-century rugs, became more popular; they were often accompanied by slogans illustrating home-spun wisdom or sentimental sayings. One shows a man asleep in a hammock with a complacent smile on his face. The caption reads MY HUSBAND IS A LAZY TRAMP AND GENERALLY NO GOOD. AND WOULD I MARRY HIM AGAIN? YOU BET YOUR LIFE I WOULD.

This Shaker rug has a characteristic geometric design and combines two techniques. The border is shirred to give a deep texture and the inner rectangle is hooked. Made between 1875 and 1885. 20x37in/52x94cm

The twentieth century brought a trend for narrative scenes, often with home-spun mottoes, such as this glimpse of daily life in rural America. 35x61in/89x155cm

Revivalism and the Arts and Crafts Movement

By the end of the nineteenth century industrialization and mass-production had brought cheap, ready-made carpets and rugs within the reach of most households. Necessity, the original spur to home rug production, had disappeared and so the craft declined. At the same time, designers who shared the ideals of William Morris deplored the loss of traditional skills and the poor quality of so many modern products. Out of this dissatisfaction the American Arts and Crafts Movement was born.

Helen Rickey Albee was one of the first of the Arts and Crafts idealists to set up hooked rug-making as a cottage industry. In 1894 she and her husband, the writer John Albee, bought an abandoned farm at Pequaket in New Hampshire. She succeeded in providing local farm women with extra income by persuading them to abandon their old designs and "their violations of good taste". She called her rugs "Abnakee" after the Abnaqui Indians from whose designs she drew inspiration. They were made with pure new wool flannel, and were often clipped.

In 1902 Lucy Thompson, a designer and architectural draughtswoman, started the Subbekashe Rug Industry in Belchertown, Massachusetts. She also based her designs on traditional Indian rugs and they were sent to Arts and Crafts exhibitions all over the country. As the century

A room at Beauport, Gloucester, Mass. showing how rag rugs achieved fashionable status in the 1920s. The house was built by Henry Davis Sleeper (*c*.1873-1934).

went on, the attempts to revive rug-making for practical and artistic purposes multiplied.

In the 1920s the Maine Seacoast Missionary Society organized rug-making among families who lived on the coast. Other home industries flourished in Tennessee, where the Pine Burr Studio produced $10,000 worth of rugs in 1930. The South End House Industry in Boston was started in 1923 and used rug-making to help town dwellers. They were supplied with all the necessary materials and paid a price per square foot for their work which was sold in Boston and at resorts nearby.

Rugs were also sold in the cities: the Colonial Revival style of decoration was all the rage and enthusiasm for old rugs was encouraged by the mistaken belief that many of them dated back to the eighteenth century; in fact few were made before 1850. As there were not enough old rugs to go round, the demand for copies grew.

Country people often sold their work from home or from stalls set up by the road. An outing to the rug-making areas of New England and Canada became a fashionable excursion for New York collectors in the 1920s and 1930s.

William Winthrop Kent, an architect and authority on antique rugs, described one such expedition:

"The hunting of the rug is going on daily," he wrote in 1930. "Literally thousands of attics and farmhouses have been searched each year in New England and Canada and the supply in many places has given out. Nova Scotia, New Brunswick, Prince Edward Island and even Labrador have sold most of their early ones.

"To see just how many could be found in a day ... the writer once took a trip into almost unknown Canadian territory as far as modern rug hunting is concerned. The journey was begun at 5.30 a.m. and lasted until dark. It covered only one hundred miles in a motor car, traversing some of the finest forests and most inspiring table-lands of one of the Canadian provinces. Wild animals darted across the road in the early mists; the scent of balsam spruce and white pine was everywhere. Before noon we had enquired along the way for rugs and rug-makers and even the postmaster helped to direct us. The farmhouses were few but neat, yet in them were found many worn rugs which the makers were glad to sell, and nowhere was a scowl or dis-courteous word encountered."

At one farm a mother and daughter tried to give him a rug, and only accepted payment on condition that the money went to charity. At another they bought "a roll of old rugs, in which we also wrapped delightful memories of Miss M. and her big brother who together ran this farm. She made many of her own rug designs excellent in pattern and colour, and if she follows my advice will never buy another design until the Canadian shop designs show improvement. Of our good designs across the border she of course knew nothing."

By the end of the day "the back of the motor was full of rugs, thirteen or fourteen, and slightly groaning". They re-crossed the river on a huge and primitive ferryboat and finally reached home well pleased with their trophies.

As time went on, more and more firms sold designs printed on hessian, as well as hooks, frames and sometimes even the material. Though ready-made designs stifled originality, they

This lively Christmas Day scene is crammed with detail and incident, including some realistic bad temper among the members of this huge family. It was made in the 1940s. 37x42in/94x107cm

In the early days of rag rug-making, life was hard and homes were draughty. The rug-makers used images of natural warmth, the sun and flowers, to help brighten the hearth. By the twentieth century, home itself was a cosy place, safe from the snow

provide an illustration of the changing tastes of the late nineteenth and early twentieth centuries. In the 1930s Burnham & Co. produced scenes of horse-drawn mail coaches which could have been taken straight from Christmas cards. Other rugs made at the time show flowers drawn in vaguely Art Deco style and even cute children with bows in their hair à la Shirley Temple.

outside which is glimpsed here through the windows of this snug and detailed 1920s sitting-room, complete with three rugs. 35x70in/90x178cm

Rug-making has enjoyed a revival in recent years – but no longer as a necessity, rather as a hobby. It is difficult, perhaps impossible, to recapture the freshness and innocence we have seen in the early examples, but on both sides of the Atlantic designers are using traditional techniques to make rag rugs which are modern in spirit.

-The British Tradition-

A classic account of working-class life in the north of England in the 1920s and 1930s describes the living-room as "the warm heart of the family ... a cluttered and congested setting, a burrow deeply away from the outside world"; here "in a few of the more careful homes" this unity of the family "is still objectified in the making of a clip-rug by the hearth. Clippings of old clothes are prepared, sorted into rough colour groups and punched singly through a piece of harding (sacking). Patterns are traditional and simple, usually a centre circle or diamond with the remainder of an unrelieved navy blue except for the edging, or that greyish-blue which most of us knew years ago in army blankets. The rug will replace at the fireside one made a long time ago and will have cost little more than the price of the harding, unless it is decided to have a vivid centre and colour is short. Then prepared clippings in, say, red, can be bought at about half a crown a pound.

"Is it to be wondered," the author Richard Hoggart concluded, "that married sons and daughters take a few years to wean themselves from their mother's hearth?"

Hoggart was remembering his childhood in Leeds, Yorkshire, in his book *The Uses of Literacy*, but the scene he described was a familiar one all over the north of England and the south of Scotland. At the time Hoggart was writing, the 1950s, the post-wartime need for economy and the slogan "Make do and mend" gave the tradition a boost, and even in the south of England, rugs continued to be made in this way into the 1970s. Rag rugs were part of both urban and rural life, as necessary in a colliery house, with its cold stone flags, as on the beaten earth floor in a farmworker's cottage.

Industrial Landscape, Ashton-Under-Lyne, by L.S. Lowry (1887-1976). Rag rug-making was never a purely rural craft and it flourished in industrial towns like this where scraps from textile mills provided an easy source of materials.

Origins

This unusually sophisticated design was made by Mrs Latymer in Northumberland in 1904.

A traditional "proddy" rug made in the south of England by Mrs Crocker, who was 93 years old in 1970. She made this at the turn of the century. 57x24in/145x60cm

If we accept that the technique has its roots in Europe, its precise origins are nonetheless lost in the distant past. The Scottish embroiderer Ann Macbeth investigated the history of rug-making in the 1920s and 1930s; she suggested ancient links with Viking settlers, pointing out that the Vikings' influence on northern England and southern Scotland is still apparent in place names, dialect words and in design. The curves and scrolls carved on furniture, for example, are similar to Scandinavian patterns and may have been copied, in turn, by rug-makers who often bordered their designs with scrolls.

As for technique, "rye" or "rya" rugs, made by pulling loops of wool through a woven backing to imitate an animal skin, were first mentioned in Swedish and Norwegian inventories and wills in about 1700. Fragments of clothes made in the same way have been found in Danish Bronze Age graves.

The Shetland Islands may have been the bridge between the two cultures, for they belonged to Norway until the fifteenth century, when they became part of Scotland under the marriage settlement of James III. The rag rug-making tradition was certainly strong there until the early years of this century and rugs were an essential part of every bride's dowry. They were often the work of "rug women" who travelled between the islands making rugs in return for hospitality.

The traditional frame used by these two Northumberland rug-makers had probably been moved out of doors especially for this photograph, which was taken in Hexham in 1875.

Rare exceptions among the mainly female rug-makers were the English and Scottish sailors who made mats by pushing short lengths of yarn or rope through a canvas backing. These "thrummed mats" were used in the rigging of their ships to stop the ropes from chafing. Poked mat-making may have been introduced into sea-faring communities via this crude version.

Rugs were made all over the British Isles but their heartland was (and still is) the ancient kingdom of Strathclyde, that is to say Britain from north Lanarkshire as far south as Morecambe Bay in Lancashire. The facts that the rugs were made in so many places and that a large number of dialect words were used to describe them point to a long history. The oral tradition takes us back to about the middle of the nineteenth century, and a rug made of uniforms worn at the Battle of Waterloo in 1815 is said to exist. The earliest dated example I have traced was made in 1863.

The rarity of old rugs is easily explained – they were not treated as heirlooms but as utilitarian objects.

A Family Pursuit

In many families it was the custom to make a new rug every winter. In country districts the frame was set up as soon as the harvest was safely in. In towns too, the long dark winter evenings were the time to get down to work. The whole family helped. The father set up the frame, and often drew the design with a charred stick from the fire. The children cut up the old clothes which had been saved all year (these were known in Cumberland as "mat clouts"). Friends and neighbours gave a hand. When the rug was finished it was laid down in front of the fire in the best room and the youngest child in the family rolled on it, though the dog or cat often got there first. The new rug was usually put down either as part of the Christmas celebrations, or when the house was spring-cleaned. Last year's hearthrug was then moved to the kitchen, that one went to the back door, and the old doormat was either thrown away or used outside – possibly in the dog-kennel or to cover the potato clamp. This three or four-year rotation meant that few rugs survived. Those that did often belonged in bedrooms where they were sometimes used as warm, if heavy, bedcovers. Lighter and brighter colours could be used upstairs, where rugs got much less worn.

A really well-made hooked rug was reversible and some house-proud owners kept them upside down, only turning them right side up on special occasions. Other families saved the best rugs for weekends. On Friday the house would be scrubbed from top to bottom and all the brass polished. The new rugs were put down for a couple of days and taken up, to be replaced by old ones on Monday morning.

In Scotland and the north of England rugs were usually made

on a frame. It made the work much quicker and easier. Old quilting frames were often used. They were up to eight feet long, heavy and cumbersome, and they used up a great deal of space in a cramped living-room. (The tradition of quilting, once as widespread as rug-making, died out in the early twentieth century, when ready-made eiderdowns became available.) In Scotland the frames were known as "stenters", from the Scottish word "stent", meaning to stretch. "Hookies" were most popu-

Made to celebrate
Queen Victoria's
Diamond Jubilee,
this rug, now in
the collection of the
Beamish Museum in
County Durham, was
rescued from a junk
shop in Carlisle, 1897.
70$^{1}/_{2}$x41$^{1}/_{2}$in/179x105cm

lar in Scotland and north-west England, though pegged rugs were also made there. In the north-east and the south of England pegged rugs were commonest. In Scotland and parts of northern England, the loops of hooked rugs were sometimes cut to give a soft pile. They were known as "clippies".

Frames were not often used in the south, though the alternative method of working on a loose hessian backing was much slower and more tiring. Another advantage of using a frame was that several people could work on it at once, for rug-making was a very sociable activity. The word would go round the village "so-and-so is putting up a pair of stenters. And we'd all go and give a hand with the new hooky".

Friends would gather, some to work on the rug, while the others would cook the food or look after the children. "Often we would sing as we matted – it was not always a gossip shop!"

Gossip and Toffee

The growth of mass-production of fabric and clothing in the nineteenth century gave a boost to rug-makers for it meant that they could purchase, cheaply and in bulk, off-cuts from mills and factories to go into their creations – a custom still current in the late 1960s as one Cumbrian rug-maker described:

"In my young days several neighbours' wives would meet and hook the rug together. We had great gossips then. The husbands worked, too, of an evening over the fire. They cut the strips, the bairns too, but they are a bit erratic and the strips have to be even, just the correct width. We used to use up all our old woollen clothes – old trousers, old stockings, old coats (washing them well of course first), but now we like using bright colours and we get bits and pieces from the woollen mills in the districts. We don't waste anything.

"Sometimes we make 'stobbie' rugs with the ends sticking out. They make warm rugs on the kitchen flags, the dogs like them, but you can't get the design so clear. Some of us are shepherds' wives and some farmers' and some cottagers'. We do the work our mothers and grandmothers taught us. The rugs last well, they are strong, they last a lifetime. You can wash them yourself but – aye – what a mess of the room when the rugmaking is on."

In towns, as in the country, cottage doors were not locked and children on their way home from school dropped in to help. "In colliery families they always had mat frames stretching away from one table to another and the whole family would be

Quilting patterns have been used for the shell shapes in this design made by Alice Graham in the mid-twentieth century.

Hessian stamped with a floral design typical of the ready-made patterns of the 1920s and 1930s.

progging away at them. Everybody had to do a turn at the mat. When you'd finished your turn somebody else took over and you got fed home-made toffee as a reward for doing ten or fifteen minutes' progging."

Hessian for backing was either bought by the yard from the draper's shop, or an old sack was washed and used. Occasionally, the sacks had on them printed trademarks, such as a chicken or a cornstook, which was an ideal ready-made design. There was keen competition for such sacks among the women on Scottish farms. Sometimes, when hessian was unobtainable, a knitted backing was used. Other possibilities were an old wool-sack, made of specially thick hessian and used for packing the farm's wool clip; hop pockets (hop sacks), which were used in Dorset had the advantage of a delicious smell. In the Second World War washed sandbags were pressed into service.

Pegged rugs, with their shaggy surface, usually had very simple designs, often with a black border made of old stockings or
men's suits. The centre was filled in with random strips known
as "hit or miss", "mixy" or, in Westmorland, "mizzy-mazzy".
Sometimes a circle or diamond shape filled the centre. Simple
stylized flower patterns were made using saucepan lids, cups
and saucers as templates. They were also outlined to make a

Black Bull rug, made in the 1960s by Mrs Janet Heap, in Cumbria, who took the idea of this majestic creature from a photograph in *Farmers' Weekly.* 34x57in/86x145cm

scalloped border, popular in Cumberland. Other patterns were derived from patchwork, such as the "crazy paving" design, or from quilting. Some families had their own templates, often based on leaves or scrolls, which were cut out of cardboard or brown paper. They were kept in a box and carefully handed down to the next generation. In the early 1920s ready-printed hessian became available. The designs were usually based on floral motifs arranged in curving borders or oval centrepieces.

The colours depended on the old clothes that were available, and were generally sombre: black, dark blue and tweed in various shades of grey or brown. In hunting country the scarlet of the "pink" coats worn by the followers of the hounds was highly sought after. Sergeants in the cavalry barracks at Leeds sold old red uniform jackets to rug-makers who liked to edge their borders with a "thin red line". In Dorset and Hampshire rag rugs were known as "soldiers' coats and sailors' trousers".

New Rugs for Old

In Cumberland there was a tradition of depicting animals on hooked rugs – it was just such a rug that inspired the interest of the painters Ben and Winifred Nicholson.

In 1923, soon after their marriage, the Nicholsons moved into a farmhouse set in the Roman Wall in Cumberland, near

Winifred's childhood home. Their next-door neighbour, a farmer's wife, Margaret Warwick, still designed and made her own rugs. She made the couple a "hookie" measuring two by four feet showing two black cats sitting on either side of a glowing fire. The traditional black border was enlivened with twelve magenta and green rosettes. The Nicholsons put it on their hearth in front of the old-fashioned black leaded range. Later, it was replaced by the large – five by three feet – "hookie" *Animal Squares* illustrated here, made by Mrs Warwick's daughter, Mary, to a design by Ben Nicholson. It had a chequer-board pattern with alternate plain and animal squares. Mary chose a

brown horse, a black collie, a turkey, a cat, a ram, a black hen, a white duck and a multi-coloured rooster. The plain squares were in Ben's favourite neutral colours except for the centre one which was made from tartan. As the Nicholsons' son Jake has pointed out, "It did not look out of place with the abstract painting by Piet Mondrian which hung on the wall."

Much later, in the 1960s, after the Nicholsons had divorced, Winifred's interest in local crafts and in Liberal Party politics was re-kindled by her neighbour, Nancy Powell, the Party agent for the constituency of Penrith and the Border. As they drove to meetings all over Cumbria they discussed ways in which they

The artist Ben Nicholson collaborated with a neighbouring farmer's daughter in Cumbria to make this unusual rug, *Animal Squares*, in the 1920s.
42x67in/106x170cm

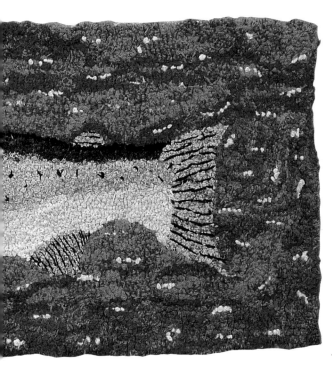

Salmon and *Footballer* were among the designs produced during the 1970s by Jake Nicholson's company, Foursquare Designs, which brought together the designs of his mother, the artist Winifred Nicholson, and the skills of the local rug-makers.

could encourage local women to use their traditional skills. Winifred's son, Jake, had a textile company, Foursquare Designs, which could market the results of the venture. It was a great success, with over one hundred and eighty rugs being made and sold in the 1970s.

Some of these "hookies" were designed by Winifred, but more were drawn by the makers themselves. Winifred was horrified by the banal ready-made patterns available in Carlisle shops, but she was equally anxious not to impose her ideas on people who, she rightly felt, were more than capable of drawing their own inspiration from the life around them. Being both a countrywoman, who had belonged to the local community all her life, and an artist, she was the ideal person to inspire the revival of a good local tradition.

Among her own designs, *Night and Day*, which forms the endpapers of this book, combines echoes of William Blake with the boldness of an inn sign, demonstrating the flair with which she could unite fine art and folk tradition. Other Foursquare designers' patterns included *Footballer*, *Cricketer*, *Scarecrow*, *Trout* and *Owl*. One complicated pattern was taken from the carving on the seventh-century cross in Bewcastle churchyard in north-east Cumbria. Some designs were drawn directly onto the backing by Winifred's grandchildren when they came to stay. Mary Warwick's two daughters, Mary Bewick and Janet Heap, drew and worked some beautiful large animal designs, sometimes including human figures and views of the distant hills as well. Janet also worked *A Knight Riding Through the Forest* which was drawn for her by Winifred Nicholson.

This Cumbrian tradition was further encouraged by Dennis and Audrey Barker of Lanercost in the 1970s. Like Winifred Nicholson, whose neighbours they were, the Barkers organized the marketing of the rugs as well as doing some designing and making, drawing inspiration from their surroundings.

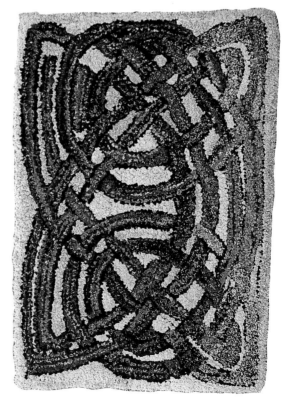

One Foursquare rug was based on the pattern carved on the seventh-century stone cross at Bewcastle church in north-east Cumbria.

Rosie in the Linen Cupboard by Louisa Creed (née Nicholson, Winifred's niece) who
used her own marmalade cat as a model, 1989. 44x34in/113x88cm

Chicken rug designed by
Emma Tennant, 1985.
24x36in/60x90cm

Joy Scott's modern hooked rug combines a traditional "crazy" pattern with a scrolled border in the style of the 1930s, when she began making rugs. 31x72in/80x182cm

English rugs which reach the level of a work of art are rare. Most are as humble in design as they are in origin. They rarely achieve the sophistication of their American counterparts. I was inspired to make rugs myself by the examples I saw in Winifred Nicholson's house a few miles from my own. My ideas come from my surroundings: out of doors there are the animals on the farm, the flowers and fruit in the garden and the views of the hills. Indoors there is the kitchen dresser or an uncontrived still-life on a table. For me one of the greatest pleasures of designing and making rugs is the way that it sharpens my perception and appreciation of even the simplest details of life.

Ma Mither's Clooty Rug
A traditional Scottish poem

Hame made it wis wi' thrifty hands
Whin the bairns they were wee,
Frae strips o' claith o' different hues,
A' matched tae plaise the ee.
Blacks and greys and blues and greens,
Wi' some rid here and there,
Cut frae a flannel petticoat
That had seen the worse for wear.
It lay afore her kitchen fire
In her wee hoose, clean and snug,
Saft and cosy on the feet,
Ma mither's clooty rug.

In winter time whin days were through
Wi' the door steekit for the nicht,
The big oil lamp set in its place
And the log fire burnin' bricht.
Ma faither drowsin' in his chair,
Nae happier could he be,
Wi' ma mither on her nursin' stail
Feedin' the bairnie on her knee,
While I lay sprawled atween them,
Me and ma collie dug,
No' a care in a' the world,
On ma mither's clooty rug.

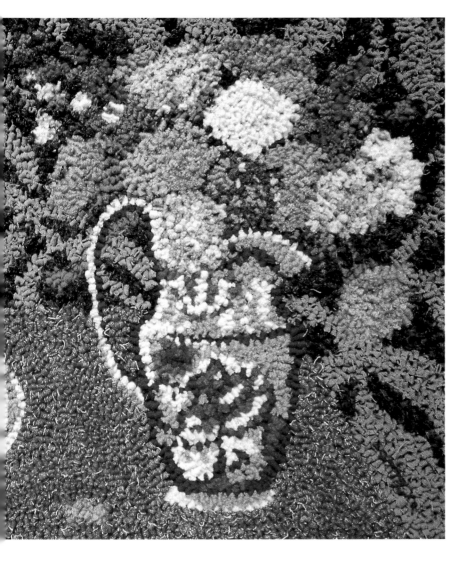

Traditional subjects given a modern treatment by Jenni Stuart-Anderson, 1987.
25x33in/64x85cm

-Canada-
Labrador and Newfoundland

When the French explorer Jacques Cartier sailed along the coast of Labrador in 1534 he reported that "the harbours are excellent, but the land is barren and fit only for wild beasts. There is not a cartload of earth in the whole country. This must be the land which God gave to Cain."

By the middle of the nineteenth century, though the coast had been settled by immigrants from the British Isles, it remained a

remote and poverty-stricken part of the British Empire. In 1892 an English doctor, Wilfred Grenfell, was sent there by the charitable Mission to Deep-Sea Fishermen. He was appalled by the harsh living conditions endured by the families who lived in villages scattered along the coast, but he loved both the place and the people, and decided to spend the rest of his life improving their lot.

In 1893 he returned to Labrador to set up the Grenfell Mission. Based in St Anthony, Newfoundland, and funded by money raised during regular lecture tours in the United States of America and Britain, the Mission built hospitals and schools, organized a team of district nurses who travelled to their patients on

A typical Grenfell rug showing the Mission boat. Made by Mrs Poole, the rug was given to Mrs Steadman, a Mission nurse, who sailed for long distances off the coast of Labrador, c.1900. 13x18in/33.5x45.5cm

Sir Wilfred Grenfell (died 1940), the missionary doctor who worked in Labrador setting up home industries, including rug-making. This photograph was taken on board ship in Labrador in about 1910.

the Mission boat and developed local industries and even built a dry-dock.

In his autobiography Grenfell recorded that "there existed on the coast the native industry of rug-hooking, to which the women were accustomed from earliest childhood. The Devonshire and Cornish and Scotch ancestors of our fisher folk must have brought out this industry with them from Old England at the same time that it migrated to New England." Grenfell was referring to the 1890s: people who were old or middle-aged then would have been born between 1820 and 1840.

Tuberculosis was rife among the fishermen's families and one of Grenfell's tasks was to teach them elementary hygiene. Spitting on the floor was a national custom – like hooking mats. So, he said, "We paid a bonus to all who would make them with 'DON'T SPIT' plainly hooked into the pattern, in place of the customary 'GOD BLESS OUR HOME'."

It was to this local skill that Grenfell turned when he was looking for a way to help the women of Labrador earn some money. He described the desperate case of a young father whom he treated for TB. Cured, but still weak, the man left hospital to go home "to a naked and half-starved family, to an empty cupboard, insufficient bed-clothing, no supplies for the fishery, no gear and no credit to get any. He had no earning capacity. What could his wife earn? This query started our industrial department."

In 1907 a volunteer arts and crafts teacher called Jessie Luther joined the Mission. Miss Luther was trained as an occupational therapist and was familiar with the work of Helen Albee in New Hampshire. She found that the local women "know the method and are technically excellent" but the mats were "very ugly in colour and design". Hitherto, the fishermen's wives had used old clothes and sometimes unravelled

Sacks printed with trade marks were a gift to the rug-makers, providing them with instant patterns. In Canada, as elsewhere, they were eagerly sought after. This rooster rug started life as a grain sack. It was made by women of the Genge family in Deadman's Cove, Strait of Belle Isle, about 1900. 37x21in/94.5x54cm

hessian, with an old sack for backing. They could dye their material in the huge cauldron filled with spruce and alder bark which the fishermen boiled up every spring. The nets were rot-proofed by being soaked in this "barking kettle", which gave them a rich dark brown colour.

Now that the bulk of the business came from selling rugs to collectors in Canada and the United States of America, standards of material and design had to be raised. Miss Luther introduced different colours and the sight of freshly-dyed material hung out to dry on the wooden fences round the Mission is still remembered. At first new flannelette was imported;

A dramatic moment from everyday life in Deadman's Cove, showing hunters and a caribou. Made by Una Way in about 1935. 23x36in/59.5x91cm

later on, in the thirties and forties, supporters of the Mission sent old silk and rayon stockings to be dyed and re-used, encouraged to do so by Grenfell's slogan: "When your stocking starts to run, let it run to Labrador".

Miss Luther was a talented designer who drew her inspiration, she said, from subjects "of local interest, being fish, ships, gulls, reindeer, Lapps, dogs, etc." Wilfred and his wife themselves designed other similar rugs. Worked in straight lines of very fine hooking and using a subtle palette, the "Grenfell" rugs are distinctive and elegant. The venture was a great success. Up to two thousand women a year were helped by the extra income they

Alice Melina Payne of Cow Head, Northern Peninsula, made this rug from a cut and folded paper pattern made for her by her mother in 1913 (*left*). 43x43in/110x110cm

This poke mat, made in Newfoundland in 1975 by Louise Belbin, shows a pattern typical of rugs in Britain. 20x35in/52x89cm

earned, and the Grenfells organized the sale of the rugs in shops in Philadelphia, New York and Ferrisburg, Vermont, as well as in Canada and England. They were labelled on the back: "Grenfell Labrador Industries. Handmade in Newfoundland and Labrador". Jessie Luther was succeeded by Rhoda Dawson, whose designs brought a modern abstract quality to the traditional motifs. Miss Dawson later returned to England, where she still lives.

South of Labrador, in Newfoundland and Nova Scotia, the rug-making tradition was equally well established. Surviving nineteenth and early twentieth-century examples have a lively sense of colour and design. Sometimes the imagery was taken from everyday life; sometimes the designs were abstract; other rugs were based on cut-out paper patterns like the snowflakes children make for Christmas decorations.

Maude O'Neill, who grew up in Newfoundland, described her mother using birch bark, onion skins and a "fungus" (more likely a kind of lichen) that grew on the rocks to make dye. She and her friends used geometric designs, which they called blocks, and they also depicted "what lived amongst them – roosters, dogs, cows, cats, boats and trees". They copied scroll patterns from lace curtains too. "I remember my mother would take a curtain with a design on it, put brown paper underneath and with a needle stab out the design. Then she would cut out the pattern and lay it on the burlap sacks." Old clothes, collected throughout the year, were the usual material but worn parts cut from seal nets were also used. Bleached by the ocean and unravelled, they made good backgrounds.

Here, as elsewhere, rug-making was traditionally a winter occupation. Maude O'Neill described how after the hooked rugs

were finished, "the last rug made each spring was called a 'Rag Jack'. You turned the frame upside down and with a pointed stick you poked holes in the burlap. All the leftover scraps were cut short and poked into the holes. This was called a 'poke mat' by some, and was used as a doormat outside for wiping feet on."

In some areas of Newfoundland these poke mats were called prodded or progged mats – the very words still used in north-east England to describe the identical method. In addition some of the designs found in Newfoundland are similar to examples from Durham and Yorkshire. One such favourite is a large diamond shape enclosed in a rectangle. The background is filled in

Similar to a Grenfell design this modern rug, Edmund Taylor's *Longliner*, brings the imagery up to date with the bright red aeroplane and a lively border that might have been inspired by an airmail envelope. It was made by Drucilla Smith of Raleigh, Northern Peninsula in 1975. 27x28in/70x71cm

with the random mixture of colours described as "scrappie" or "hit or miss".

Ready-made designs, usually consisting of scrolls and stylized flowers, were available by 1900. They were called "stamped mats" in Newfoundland. The same motifs are often found in different combinations because women would trace off part of a neighbour's bought design and adapt it to their taste.

But original designs were still made. In 1928, an article in *The House Beautiful* quoted a woman in Nova Scotia who described how she got the idea for a rug she had made with a black cat on a red background:

"I wanted something to draw on a rug, and I couldn't find anything. I looked in the yard and after a while I saw our cat, Malty, and I said to myself, 'He'll be good enough.' Then I got my old man to hold him down on this piece of burlap while I drew round him with a pencil. But I didn't know what to do with his tail. He was lying on it, so it didn't show in the picture. But no cats grow without tails, so my old man held it out nice and straight, then I just stuck it on here."

Fashionable Folk Rugs

Rug-making in Canada was given a boost by the growing demand from collectors in the United States. Similar Arts and Crafts style manufacture also developed, most notably under the influence of Mrs Alexander Graham Bell. The Bells acquired a house on Cape Breton Island in Nova Scotia at the end of the nineteenth century. Like Wilfred Grenfell in Labrador, Mrs Bell was impressed by the skill of the local rug-makers but not by the garish colours they used. She brought in an artist, Lilian Burke, to improve the quality of design and organize a home industry, to be known as the Cheticamp Hooked Rug Industry.

Miss Burke specialized in subtly-coloured floral patterns, but she was not afraid to work on the grand scale. One rug, made at Cheticamp in 1938 for a New York client measured eighteen

by thirty-six feet and took eight women six months to make. The elaborate design was adapted by Miss Burke from a Savonnerie rug in the Louvre. In 1939 an article in *The Christian Science Monitor* said that the Cheticamp industry was "catering to New York decorators who order rugs to be used in palatial homes". It also said that "in many homes rug earnings bring in the only actual cash that is seen year-round".

The maritime provinces of Canada shared a common culture with New England across the border and the rugs made there are very similar. The Canadians made use of their traditional motifs, the maple leaf and the beaver, and were more inclined to

Abigail Smith's rug
of 1860, the earliest
dated Canadian rug
to survive.
29x52in/74x132cm

mix materials, such as cotton, linen and unravelled hessian, than their New England counterparts, who usually kept to pure wool.

Rugs were also made further west in Ontario and Quebec. An example from Ontario dated 1885 shows a duck, not in this case drawn from life, but from a wooden decoy.

The earliest dated Canadian rug to survive was made in New Maryland in 1860 by Abigail Smith. Her sophisticated design resembles the finest New England examples.

On the vexed question of the origins of rug-hooking, the evidence in Canada is incomplete and somewhat contradictory. While it might seem reasonable to assume that it was the British settlers who first introduced it, rug-making has a long history among French Canadians who could not have brought the technique from France as there is no tradition there. One possible explanation may be that the French Canadian rug-makers took their inspiration originally from embroidery. Among the earliest French settlers in Canada were several orders of nuns. The Ursulines, for example, were established there in the 1690s. They kept alive a vast repertoire of traditional French designs. Sophisticated floral embroideries on priestly garments and altar-frontals would have been seen by rural settlers every Sunday in church, and they may have been inspired to copy them in their own, very different, medium which may have been derived from tambour-stitch embroidery.

Early "Acadian" rugs made by these French settlers in what is now Nova Scotia and Cape Breton Island used the yarn-sewn technique. Often the rug was clipped so as to raise the design against the background. These rugs, which usually had elaborate floral designs influenced later hooked rugs made in the similarly shaggy "Waldoboro" technique.

Nineteenth-Century Canadian Rug Rhyme

I am the family wardrobe, best and worst
Of all generations, from the first;
Grandpa's Sunday-go-to-meetin' coat,
And the woollen muffler he wore at his throat;
Grandma's shawl, that came from Fayal;
Ma's wedding gown, three times turned and once let down,
Which once was plum but now turned brown;
Pa's red flannels, that made him itch;
Pants and shirts; petticoat and skirts;
From one or another, but I can't tell which.
Tread carefully, because you see, if you scuff me,
You scratch the bark of the family tree.

-Further Reading-

American Hooked and Sewn Rugs, Joel and Kate Kopp, E.P. Dutton and Co. Inc., New York, USA, 1975.

American Rugs and Carpets from the 17th Century to Modern Times, Helene Van Rosenstiel, Barrie and Jenkins, London, 1978.

American Textiles and Needlework, Sheila Betterton, American Museum, Bath, 1977.

At Home in Upper Canada, Jean Minhinnick, Clarke, Irwin and Co., Vancouver and Toronto, Canada, 1970.

The Hooked Rug: A Record, Tudor Publishing Co., New York, USA, 1937.

Mat Making in the North-East, Tyne & Wear County Council Museums Service information sheet, Tyne and Wear, 1980.

The Nicholsons: A Story of Four People and Their Designs, catalogue of exhibition, York City Art Gallery, York, 1988.

Rag Rugs in the Somerset Rural Life Museum, Mary Gryspeerdt, unpublished thesis, SRLM, 1982.

Ragtime, Diane Gilder, catalogue of an exhibition held at the Shipley Art Gallery, Gateshead, Tyne and Wear, 1988.

Rare Hooked Rugs, William Winthrop Kent, Pond-Ekberg Company, Springfield, Mass., USA, 1941.

Romance of Labrador and *Forty Years for Labrador*, Sir Wilfred Grenfell, Hodder and Stoughton, London.

Shaker Textile Arts, Gordon Beverly, University Press of New England, USA, 1980.

Unknown Colour: Paintings, Letters and Writings, Winifred Nicholson, Faber and Faber, London, 1987.

-Glossary of Rugging Terms-

The words "mat" and "rug" as used in this book are synonymous. Mat was the more common term in north-east England and eastern Canada, and rug was more usual elsewhere. Terms for hooked and poked rugs vary from place to place.

Region	Hooked	Pegged
Somerset and Devon	Looped	Shaggy or Peggy
Wales	Hookie	Proddie
East Cumbria		Tabbie
Cumbria		Stobbie/Stobbed
Westmoreland		Brodded
Co. Durham		Proggie/progged
Yorkshire		Tatty
Scotland	Clootie, Cleikie, Hookie	Proddy or Peggie
Berwick on Tweed		Probby
United States	Hooked/Drawn in	Poked
Labrador/ Newfoundland	Hooked	Poked/Prodded

Bodger: English Midlands term for rug-poking tool.

Brin: Canadian term for hessian backing.

Burlap: American term for hessian backing.

Caterpillar or Chenille rugs: made in the first half of the nineteenth century by sewing strips of material down the middle and pulling the stitches to gather the surface into loops – also known as shirring.

Clippy: a hooked rug, cut to form a soft pile. Confusingly, the same word was used in Yorkshire, Durham and Northumberland to describe a rug made by the pegging method.

Harding: Yorkshire term for hessian backing.

Linsey-woolsey: mixture of home-spun linen and wool used for backing rugs in the USA before 1850.

Pogger: Wiltshire term for rug-poking tool.

Sheared: a hooked rug with the loops clipped to give a soft pile (see **clippy**).

Shirring: see **caterpillar**.

Stenters: Scottish term for rug-stretching frame.

Stobber: East Cumbrian term for rug-poking tool.

1885 rug made by Polly Eldridge Miner in Bridport, Vermont. A rare example of an American rug made by the pegged or poked technique. 34x19in/86x47cm

-Places to Visit-

Great Britain

Abbot Hall Art Gallery
80 Wigton Road
Kendal
Cumbria

American Museum
Claverton Manor
Bath
Avon BA2 7BD

Beamish Open Air Museum
Beamish
Nr. Chester-le-Street
Co. Durham DH9 0RG

Dove Cottage & the Wordsworth
Museum
Town End
Grasmere
Cumbria

Museum of East Anglian Life
Stowmarket
Suffolk

East Riddlesden Hall
Bradford Road
Keighley
Yorkshire BD20 5EL

Highland Folk Museum
Duke Street
Kingussie
Inverness

Ryedale Folk Museum
Hutton-le-Hole
York

Somerset Rural Life Museum
Abbey Farm
Chilkwell Street
Glastonbury
Somerset BA6 8DB

Shipley Art Gallery
Prince Consort Road
Gateshead
Tyne & Wear

Ulster Folk & Transport Museum
153 Bangor Road
Holywood
Northern Ireland

United States of America

Henry Ford Museum
20900 Oakwood Blvd
Dearborn, MI 48121

Wenham Historical
Association Museum
132 Main Street
Wenham, MA 01984

Shelburne Museum
Route 7
Shelburne, VT 05482

Currier Gallery of Art
192 Orange Street
Manchester, NH 03104

Essex Institute Museum
132 Essex Street
Salem, MA 01970

Museum of American Folk Art
49 West 53rd Street
New York, NY 10019

Beauport, The Sleeper McCann
House
75 Eastern Point Blvd
Gloucester, MA 01930

Hancock Shaker Village
Route 20
Pittsfield Albany Road
Pittsfield, MA 01202

Shakertown
Pleasant Hill
Kentucky

Shaker Museum
95 Shaker Museum Road
Old Chatham, NY 12136

Canada

Museum for Textiles
55 Centre Avenue
Toronto, ON M5G 2H5

New Brunswick Museum
277 Douglas Avenue
Saint John
NF A1C 5S7

McCord Museum of Canadian
History
690 Sherbrooke Street
W Montreal, PQ H3A 1E9

Grenfell Handicrafts
PO Box 280
St Anthony
Newfoundland

Charlottetown Confederation
Centre Art Gallery
Charlottetown, PE C1A 7L9

Memorial University Art Gallery
Arts and Cultural Centre
St John's, NF A1C 5S7

Art Gallery of Nova Scotia
1741 Hollis Street
PO Box 2262
Halifax, NS B3J 3C8

-Acknowledgements-

I became interested in the history of rag rugs through making them myself. I doubt if I would have persevered without the support of many friends. I am especially grateful to Elizabeth Glenconner and Nancy Lancaster.

Many people have helped me write this book. Mrs Diane Gilder of the Shipley Art Gallery, Gateshead, shared with me her deep knowledge of the subject. The exhibition of rugs, "Ragtime", which was held at the Shipley in 1988, was a landmark in the appreciation of rag rugs in this country.

The late Winifred Nicholson inspired me to make rugs. Her sons Jake and Andrew have been a valuable link with the past and provided much information. I also enjoyed talking to their one-time nanny, Janet Heap and to Mrs Nicholson's niece, Jennifer Steinbugler.

Others who have taken trouble on my behalf are Jill Betts of the Museum of Rural Life, Reading; Alice and Mary Keen; Rosanna James; Rosemary Allen of the North of England Open Air Museum, Beamish; Shelagh Ford and Sheila Betterton of the American Museum, Bath; Janet Dugdale of Abbot Hall, Kendal; John Cornforth; Christine Birch; Sally Coomer and her sister Joan Yeomans, whose knowledge of rug-making in Canada was very useful; Helen Joseph of the Shipley Art Gallery; E.Q. Nicholson; Irene Waters; A.J. McCarthy of the Wordsworth Trust; Linda Ballard of the Ulster Folk and Transport Museum; Christine Stevens of the Welsh Folk Museum; Mrs McAlister of the Angus Folk Museum; Eleanor Thompson of Wenham Museum, Mass.; Joan Moshimer; Vicki Weissman; and Peter Laroque of the New Brunswick Museum.

I have learnt a great deal from the members of the many Women's Institutes, Church Guilds and Scottish Rural Institutes at which I have demonstrated rug-making.

Nearer home, I must thank Jean Elliot, Jenny Harkness and Edna Sinclair, who has typed my manuscript.

Finally, Mirabel Cecil asked me to write this book. For that idea, and for all the work that she, her co-editor, Rosemary Hill, and their colleagues at Walker Books have done, my grateful thanks. Any mistakes are mine alone.

Snail by Jenni Stuart-Anderson. 31in/79cm diameter

-About the Author-

Emma Tennant lives in Roxburghshire, Scotland, a few miles from the border with Cumberland where Winifred Nicholson lived in a house set into the Roman Wall. She is married to a farmer. She spends the winters making rag rugs and designing

rugs which are made by a group of her neighbours and market-
ed under the name Hermitage Rugs. She spends the summer
painting flowers in her studio at the foot of the Cheviot Hills,
and is a member of the Council of the National Trust.

Kitchen Dresser with Daisies
by Emma Tennant, 1987.
24x36in/61x91cm

-Picture Credits-

Our thanks are due to:

Abbot Hall Art Gallery, Kendal
Page 59

America Hurrah, NYC, USA
Pages 28, 38, 40-41, 46-47, 70 (left)

American Museum in Britain, Bath
Cover, pages 14, 16, 19, 24, 25, 26, 30, 35, 36, 37

North of England Open Air Museum, Beamish
Frontispiece, pages 50, 52, 54, 57 (below)

Christine Birch
Page 12

Patrick Benson
Pages 32-33

Bradford Art Gallery and Museums/Bridgeman Art Library
Page 49

Richard Cheek
Page 43

Metropolitan Museum of Art, New York, USA. Sansbury-Mills Fund, 1961
Page 22

New Brunswick Museum, St John, Newfoundland, Canada
Pages 80-81

Memorial University of Newfoundland, Canada
Pages 73, 74, 75, 76, 77, 78

Museum of English Rural Life, Reading
Pages 50, 70 (right)

Shelburne Museum, Vermont, USA
Pages 20, 45, 84

Shipley Art Gallery, Gateshead. Reproduced by arrangement with Tyne & Wear Museums
Endpapers, pages 57 (above), 60, 62 (below), 66 (above), 87

Jenni Stuart-Anderson
Pages 13, 69, 91

Ken Taylor
Pages 17, 18, 62 (above), 64

Emma Tennant
Pages 10, 66 (below), 92

Wenham Historical Society, Wenham, USA
Page 29

-The Decorative Arts Library-

Early English Porcelain
Bevis Hillier

Modern Block Printed Textiles
Alan Powers

Point Engraving on Glass
Laurence Whistler

Rag Rugs of England and America
Emma Tennant

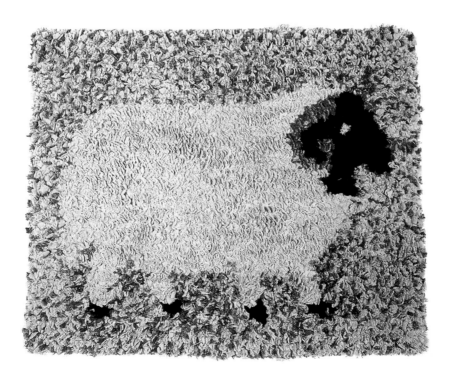

Shaggy Sheep rug made in Cumbria in 1984 by Jean Little and designed by Denis Barker. 39x31½in/100x80cm